THIS JOURNAL BELONGS TO

....

ZEN
MEDITATIONS
Journal

MEDITATIONS AND PROMPTS FOR LIVING
A SIMPLE, HAPPY, AND PEACEFUL LIFE

The Hay House Editors

HAY HOUSE, INC.
Carlsbad, California • New York City
London • Sydney • New Delhi

INTRODUCTION

WELCOME TO YOUR
ZEN MEDITATIONS JOURNAL!

The school of Zen has been around for over a thousand years. A branch of Buddhism, it started in India and traveled to China and then Japan, where its focus on meditation as a way to profound revelation was warmly and widely embraced. In the centuries since, it has spread around the globe, where different cultures, religions, and individuals have adopted and adapted it. Today you can still find its ideas explored in temples and monasteries, but you'll also come across them in yoga studios, spas, museums, and even stores.

Indeed, the word *Zen* has expanded to mean many things to many people. These days, when people in the West hear it, they often think of a peaceful state of mind, perhaps unruffled by the outside world, before they think of monks in robes. Maybe this seems like "real" Zen has been diluted, but Zen has always aimed to see the true nature of creation, unperturbed by its messiness and contradictions, especially those in human thought.

It has been called a philosophy and a religion, and it is and isn't those things. It's about seeing through the logic and stories and feelings we create about the world to how reality really is—beyond words and thought. It's about finding peace and even

enjoyment in what can't be known. It's about being fully present in the moment. It's about seeing that any separateness from creation that you feel as an individual is an illusion. It's about creating a state of openness and awareness instead of reflection and projection. It is obvious and it's a mystery. It's a lot of things and it's one thing. It's all these things and none of these things. It's complicated and it's simple.

That may sound like a lot! But rest assured, this journal aims to take you on a simple journey. You'll explore traditional Zen Buddhist ideas like beginner's mind, mindfulness, compassion, nonviolence, and koans as well as more modern, secular Zen ideas about joy, laughter, flow, and gratitude. Take what you like and leave the rest! This is your journal journey after all.

Through all the exercises, allow your writing, drawing, and coloring to just flow. Try not to worry about logic, structure, grammar, or spelling. Don't edit yourself and, as best you can, don't judge yourself for what you write. Allow your hand to just go as you free-write, guided by your intuition. In this way, you'll grow to know your true nature and the joy that comes with such knowing, which is what Zen is all about.

FIND *YOUR* ZEN

While the word *Zen* is a centuries-old term that literally means "meditation" or "thought," it has taken on many meanings in modern English. From the name of a religious school to a state of calm to a way to describe decor, Zen is everywhere these days, bringing to mind different things for different people.

What does Zen mean to you? Trust your intuition as you write.

....

....

....

....

....

....

....

....

....

THE JOY OF BEING

*f*inding joy in the fact that you exist is one of the great goals of Zen meditation. Being fully present in each moment, aware that it is a miracle to exist at all, is central to the work and the reward of Zen. So simple, yet so not simple.

Free-write on this idea and what emotions it brings up for you.

....

....

....

....

....

....

....

....

....

....

....

"IF YOUR MIND IS EMPTY,
IT IS ALWAYS READY FOR
ANYTHING; IT IS OPEN
TO EVERYTHING. IN THE
BEGINNER'S MIND THERE
ARE MANY POSSIBILITIES;
IN THE EXPERT'S MIND
THERE ARE FEW."

–Shunryu Suzuki

BEGINNER'S MIND

At the heart of Zen practice is developing the "beginner's mind." This is a way of thinking that tries to approach the world without prejudice or prejudgment. It encourages you to try to experience everything as if for the first time, as a beginner, even things you might feel you're an expert on. This frees you from old habits and preconceived notions, allowing you to doubt what you think you know and joyfully discover the true nature of things.

To foster the beginner's mind, first ask yourself, Who am I? Try to step outside of yourself and consider this question at the most basic level—with the beginner's mind.

....

....

....

....

....

....

....

....

continued . . .

FREE YOURSELF

We all have habits, good and bad. And not just habitual actions like saying please and thank you or biting our nails. We also have habits of mind in the ways we think and feel about the world around us and ourselves. Fostering a beginner's mind helps you break out of your patterned way of thinking to see deeper truths and open you up to new possibilities.

What is something you think about often, or an emotional reaction you're prone to feeling? What are the triggers for this habit of mind? What are some ways you can respond to these triggers that break free from your habitual reactions? Try to think of them from a child's perspective, with a sense of lightness and play.

WIDE-EYED

*O*nce you start to think about the world with a beginner's mind, you may find you begin to understand things from the point of view of others. One way to do this is to ask a question, such as "Should people eat meat?" and answer it in different ways: yes, no, and maybe. Even if you don't ultimately agree with the answers you come up with, a beginner's mind shows you things from all perspectives and allows you to get closer to the true nature of things even as your empathy grows.

Think about a question you hold a deep opinion about and try to reapproach it with a beginner's mind. Answer it yes, no, and maybe as best you can below.

THE DON'T-KNOW MIND

The beginner's mind shows us that while the expert's mind is closed, the child's mind is open to possibility. The don't-know mind is similar but perhaps goes one step further. It asks you to consider that despite your desire to know things, there is little that you can *really* know. Where does life come from? What happens in death? What will the future be? If you start from the fluid place of "I don't know" for questions big and small, instead of in the static and potentially false place of "I know," you become open to the true nature of things. Fear of the unknown eases as you come to understand that "knowing" blocks out the truth.

Write down as many things you can think of that you don't know.

....

....

....

....

....

....

....

FIND YOUR SEAT

Traditionally, Zen meditation is done sitting in the lotus position with the hands forming a mudra in the lap, as shown in the illustration, in which you rest one hand in the other, both palms up, with your thumb tips touching to form an oval. Today, however, most meditation  teachers recommend meditating in a simple crossed-leg position that is comfortable and easy. Indeed, there are a number of seated postures you can use to meditate, some more challenging than others. Finding the most comfortable position for you and your needs is key to developing a meditation practice you enjoy sticking with. Here are some traditional options:

Lotus: Cross-legged with your feet on top of your thighs, sitting on a cushion

Half Lotus: Cross-legged with one foot on top of a thigh and the other below

Burmese: Cross-legged with both feet on the ground, not under the thighs

Seiza Using a Stool: A kneeling posture in which you sit on a stool with your feet under it

Seiza Using a Chair: A kneeling posture in which you sit on a cushion with your feet on either side of it

Support your body however it needs it. For example, you can consider lying down to meditate or using a lumbar support pillow in a chair. No matter how you position yourself, keep your spine straight. Imagine you are being pulled by a string from the top of your head; it keeps your spine straight as your shoulders hang relaxed off this central pillar.

Sketch yourself here in happy meditation.

"WE WATCH THE BREATH UNTIL WE BECOME THE BREATH. IN THIS WAY, AS IT IS SAID IN ZEN, WE COME TO KNOW THE BREATH, OURSELVES, AND ALL THINGS INTIMATELY."

–Joan Duncan Oliver

ZAZEN

*O*ne of the core practices of Zen is, of course, meditation. Zazen refers to the seated meditation practiced in Zen Buddhism; it blends both concentration and relaxation, form and void. It is a study of the self so you may forget the self.

To practice zazen, simply sit with your back straight and muscles relaxed, one hand resting in the other. With eyes gazing softly at the ground in front of you (the traditional way) or closed, focus your thoughts on your breath. Allowing your face to rest in a slight smile may help you relax. Allow your mind to follow the breath, in and out. Count one when you inhale, one when you exhale; two when you inhale, two when you exhale; and so on, up to ten and down again.

Your mind will wander. Acknowledge these wanderings gently and without judgment, then focus on the breath, starting again at one. So simple, yet so difficult. But rest assured, the more you meditate, the easier and more beneficial it becomes.

Meditate for 15 minutes, or as long as you're comfortable doing so, and then write about your experience.

....

....

....

....

continued . . .

What emotions came up as you sat?

....

....

....

....

....

....

How do you feel now, compared with before you meditated?

....

....

....

....

....

....

....

....

ZEN OUT COLORING

GO TO GROUND

*A*ny time you're feeling spun out by anxiety, scattered by too many demands, or otherwise lost, confused, or overwhelmed, you can use the basic tools of meditation to ground yourself. First, you have to notice that you're ungrounded. That's something meditation will help you recognize earlier and earlier, before you become entirely spun out. Try to identify the sensations you are experiencing and where they are located in your body. Then bring your attention to your breath and count the inhales and exhales, up to 10, just as if you were sitting to meditate. Focus on the feeling of the air traveling through your nose and lungs and the sensation of your chest and stomach rising and falling.

Write a few lines about how you're feeling right now. Then try this grounding meditation and write about how you feel after it.

....

....

....

....

....

....

DRIFTING CLOUDS

When you first practice meditating, you will likely find your thoughts darting all about. Instead of peacefulness and clarity, you may feel frustration or stress as you sit. This is a normal and natural experience. Instead of chasing those thoughts down, giving them a story and importance, try to just acknowledge them and then let them pass by, like clouds drifting past the sun. The more you meditate, the easier this becomes, and the more you'll experience this nonattachment to unbidden thoughts even when you're not sitting.

Meditate for 15 minutes, or however long you're comfortable. Allow your thoughts to just pass by. Below, write about what came up for you, then on the next page draw your experience.

REFLECT

Now that you've been exploring Zen for a bit, take some time to reflect on your experience.

Has anything changed for you, in your life, your mind, or your habits? Have you had any realizations or revelations? What intentions do you have for your journey forward?

....

....

....

....

....

....

....

....

....

....

ZEN KOANS CAN GIVE YOU A HAND

A koan is a seemingly simple statement or question that is meant to help you see a greater truth. It might be a riddle or a paradox. It might even seem silly or easily answered at first, but careful consideration can reveal something deeply true or something that can only be understood by the heart instead of the logical brain.

You've almost certainly heard one of the most famous koans but didn't realize it was first posed by an 18th-century Japanese Zen monk: What is the sound of one hand clapping? This question is probably so familiar to you that it seems like a joke or a cliché, but it's also probable that you've never really considered it.

Really reflect on this koan, doing your best to come at it with a beginner's mind.

....

....

....

....

....

....

Sketch what comes to mind when you think of the sound of one hand clapping.

ACTING OUT ALL IS ONE

A key idea in traditional Zen Buddhism is that all creation is one. The separateness you feel as an individual—that you are in some way isolated or discrete from the rest of creation—is understood as a product of the imagination. All things are actually interconnected in one eternal existence—a somewhat simple and obvious truth that is nonetheless difficult to internalize.

In your day-to-day life, what are some actions you can take that embrace the idea that all is one?

....

....

....

....

....

....

....

....

"THE FINGER THAT
POINTS AT THE MOON
IS NOT THE
MOON ITSELF."

–Thich Nhat Hanh

BEYOND IDEAS

Meditating on the oneness of creation may sound like an intellectual or philosophical pursuit, but it is at once bigger and simpler than that. Meditating on this idea is what points you to true reality, to *feel* the connection with all things, instead of just understanding it in an abstract way. It is not a rigorous doctrine you need to analyze and defend. It is not the truth itself. It is an idea that guides you to the true nature of things, which is beyond concepts and intellectual understanding.

Spend some time meditating on the idea of oneness, then write about how this meditation felt. Did you feel, if only for a second, the truth of this idea? Are there other things that you feel the truth of rather than know them?

....

....

....

....

....

....

....

continued . . .

WAIT, JUST LISTEN

A listening meditation connects you to the reality around you. It helps you become more mindful of your space and all that is happening around you that you often don't even notice. The sounds of the house settling and working, traffic in the distance, birds outside the window. Even if you're in a quiet space, there are always the sounds of the world going about its business.

Today, sit in meditation and bring your attention to the sounds around you. Then write about all the things you heard and how this meditation felt.

....

....

....

....

....

....

....

....

MIND YOUR ZEN

Mindfulness, like many things in Zen, is the simplest thing in the world, but it can also be oh-so-difficult in practice. Being mindful is just being aware of your present moment. You are here and now, experiencing things with all your senses, instead of doing what we all usually do, which is barely paying attention to our surroundings as we tap away on some technology and worry about a million things, past and present. So simple in theory, so hard to do.

Achieving a mindful state is the heart of Zen. This is so simple in theory, yet so hard to do. As we've already explored, it's key to meditation—becoming aware of your breathing, your self, and your interconnectedness with creation—but you can bring that mindful alertness to any moment in your life. This can help break you out of a cycle of worry and ground you or just help you appreciate something awesome that's going on around you. (It doesn't mean you can never think about the future or plan ahead, but when you're doing that, do that. Try not to do that in the background as you do everything else.)

Practice some mindful awareness now by taking a moment to become aware of everything around you. Write about your here and now and try to incorporate all your senses.

....

....

....

HAPPY PLACE

Mindfulness is more than a meditative practice. It's a state of awareness, a way of being that you can embrace any moment of any day. The more you call on it, the more you make it into a habit, the more peaceful you will feel, and the deeper your Zen practice will become. One of the easiest times to practice mindfulness is when you're in your happy place, whether that's walking your favorite trail, snuggling in your favorite comfy spot at home, visiting your favorite people, or all of the above. When you're doing something you love, why not savor it as best you can, paying attention to all the details and your presence within them? Be conscious of every breath you take, every movement of your body, and every thought and feeling that you have.

Make time to visit one of your happy places today and practice mindful awareness when you're there. Then write about the experience. Did you notice anything new?

....

....

....

....

....

JUST DO THE DISHES

While it's easy to see how being mindful while you're in your happy place can make the experience even better, the same is true for your daily chores. It might seem that being super aware of scrubbing a gunky pot might be the opposite of what you want to do, but being mindful of your actions and focusing only on what you are doing (instead of planning or worrying or begrudging or sending your thoughts elsewhere from where you are) creates a feeling of appreciation and connection that's better than distraction. You can find joy in all of life's moments if you start from the simple point of appreciating that you're alive.

When you do the dishes (or some other chore) today, just do the dishes. Be mindful of your breath, the feel of the water, the act itself, then write about how doing the dishes while fully present was different from how you normally do them.

....

....

....

....

....

....

"IF WE CHOOSE TO DRINK A CUP OF TEA IN MINDFULNESS, THE PLEASURE OF DRINKING TEA WILL MORE THAN DOUBLE BECAUSE WE ARE TRULY THERE AND THE TEA IS ALSO TRULY THERE."

–Thich Nhat Hanh

MAKE TEA A MEDITATION

Taking the time to deeply appreciate the act of brewing and drinking tea has been an important part of Zen Buddhism for centuries and is something you may enjoy bringing into your own daily practice. Paying complete attention as you boil the water, steep the tea, and sip it is mindfulness in action. If you treat it with this reverence, you make it a ritual that enhances not just the experience of the tea itself, but also your state of mind and inner peace. Mindfully drinking tea also lends itself to meditating on the interconnectedness of all things.

Brew yourself some tea and think about how the difference between subject and object, you and the tea, melts away as you drink the tea and it becomes part of you.

....

....

....

....

....

....

....

continued . . .

WABI-SABI AND THE ART OF ZEN

In Zen, you focus on the moment at hand instead of fixating on the past or future, and you embrace reality for what it is instead of wishing it were otherwise. The idea of wabi-sabi is, in a sense, seeing exactly that in an object. It's the act of finding beauty in things even and especially when those things are simple, maybe a little worn out, and imperfect.

Wabi-sabi started out as two different ideas in Japanese aesthetics. *Wabi* was originally a word that indicated isolation and loneliness, but in the 15th century, it came to mean a sort of subdued beauty that was minimal and maybe even severe, something that is simple and rustic and quiet and, in those ways, beautiful. This meaning grew out of a time when art and objects in Japan were becoming increasingly lavish and opulent. Wabi was a Zen call back to simplicity and nature.

The word *sabi* refers to the tarnish and cracks that appear in objects over time, the patina of age that appears on a metal bowl or the crackle in the glaze of a well-used teacup. Over the centuries *sabi* came to mean not just these "imperfections" that come from age but also the beauty and appreciation you can find in these so-called imperfections.

Today, *wabi-sabi* is most often used as one term to talk about the paradoxical perfect beauty found in imperfection. It celebrates imperfection, change, reality on reality's terms, and the idea that simple, modest things capture the real and complex beauty of creation.

Draw something you cherish that captures wabi-sabi—that is, beautiful in its age or imperfection.

MONKEY MIND

*Y*ou may have heard the term *monkey mind* in reference to to racing thoughts that restlessly swing all over the place, confused and indecisive and always wanting something. This may seem like a modern state of mind, but it is in fact a Buddhist idea that goes back many centuries. It might seem like the monkey mind is the enemy of mindfulness, but the Zen approach is not to struggle with your monkey mind but to befriend it. Without judgment, gently accept that this is how minds work, and then you can observe the swinging monkey with a sense of friendliness, even enjoyment.

This doesn't, however, mean you give the monkey shiny things to play with and encourage it to rampage around, which in these days could mean engaging with devices and multitasking. Instead, give it a calm space to settle down in—that is, meditation and mindfulness. The more meditation you practice and the more intention and awareness you bring to all you do, the calmer and happier the monkey of your mind will be.

When does your monkey mind swing into high gear? By writing about what triggers it, you become more aware of these triggers and can call on the mindfulness techniques of breathing and awareness before the monkey gets out of control.

....

....

....

WHERE DO YOU THINK YOU'RE GOING?

$\mathcal{S}$itting in meditation is all about focusing your mind, and as it wanders, which it naturally and inevitably does, bringing it back to focus. That *is* meditation. Noticing where your mind goes when you meditate can help you get to know yourself, and it can also help you improve your focus. Once you become aware of the paths your mind tends to wander down, you can begin to catch yourself before venturing too far down them.

Get into your favorite position and meditate for however long you're currently comfortable with. Afterward, write about where your mind tended to go.

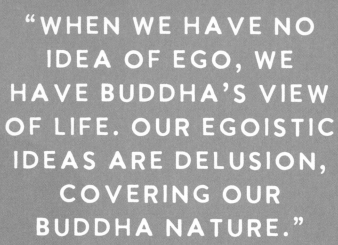

"WHEN WE HAVE NO
IDEA OF EGO, WE
HAVE BUDDHA'S VIEW
OF LIFE. OUR EGOISTIC
IDEAS ARE DELUSION,
COVERING OUR
BUDDHA NATURE."

–Shunryu Suzuki

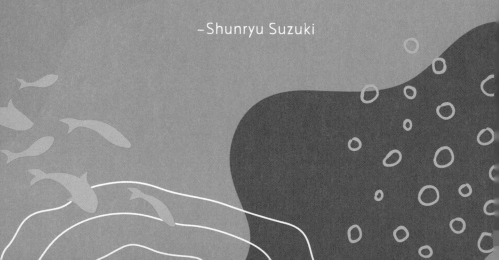

INNER GOLD

*A*ccepting and trusting yourself as you are is itself inner peace, but getting caught up in worrying about what you think are your flaws and what you think you should be instead is part of human nature. It's like the story of the golden Buddha statue that monks covered in concrete to protect it from being plundered by an invading army. The monks are driven off, but their ploy works and the statue is left alone. It's forgotten and stays covered in concrete for many, many years after the war is over, until one day a monk meditating near it sees a chunk of stone fall away and realizes the Buddha is made of gold, not concrete. We do this all the time. We become wrapped up in the things the world puts on us and forget our true self, the Buddha nature hidden underneath.

What are some things you feel wrapped up in that hide your true, golden nature?

....

....

....

....

....

....

continued . . .

ZEN OUT COLORING

WE ARE ONE

Just as we need to learn to accept that we are at one with the perfection of creation to find inner peace, we need to extend that same love and understanding to others. We are so prone to seeing the "imperfections" in people, to judgment, but when we can put that down and learn to love people for who they are, for the unity we have with them, then we can be at peace. Then we start to experience the true nature of things.

Think of someone who has annoyed you recently and try meditating for a few minutes on their true nature and how you and they are actually one. Then write about how your feelings changed (or didn't!) from before to after your meditation.

BRIDGE BUILDING

*O*ne aspect of feeling you are in Zen harmony is when your outer life reflects your inner life. If you think one thing and do another, that's bound to make you feel mixed up. For instance, if you burn to be creative but never give yourself time or permission to create, that doesn't feel great. If it's important to you to treat everyone with respect but then you're dismissive of someone who annoys you, that makes you feel kind of yucky, doesn't it? The sturdier the bridge you build between the person you are on the inside and the things you do on the outside, the more harmony you'll feel with your true nature.

Write down some things that you feel inwardly but act outwardly in a different way.

....

....

....

How can you build the bridge stronger, so your inner and outer parts better align with one another?

IF YOU ARE TIRED . . .

*R*est. Life, responsibilities, to-do lists, even thoughts can feel overwhelming. In times of stress and weariness, it's easy to believe that you need to keep pushing forward, to keep going, to keep working or you'll never get it all done. The truth, however, is that if you don't rest, you'll never get it all done.

When you feel mentally or physically tired, it's important to listen to yourself, to trust the messages you're sending yourself, and to honor your feelings by resting. This can be as simple as taking a few purposeful breaths until you feel calm and centered, sitting in meditation for a few minutes, or going for a walk in which you're mindfully attentive to the present moment.

What is your energy level right now?

Take five minutes of rest right now in which, no matter what you choose to do, you do it mindfully and intentionally. What is your energy level now?

How do you feel after your intentional rest?

REFLECT

*T*ake some time to reflect on your experience exploring Zen over the course of this journal.

Has anything changed for you, in your life, your mind, or your habits? Have you had any realizations or revelations? What intentions do you have for your journey forward?

....

....

....

....

....

....

....

....

....

....

DIGITAL DECOMPRESSION

All our glowing, flashing, ringing, pinging devices are distractions from maintaining mindfulness. Just when you're really feeling immersed in the beauty of a sunset, your phone buzzes or you think to yourself, *I should get a picture of this!* Just as you finish pouring yourself a cup of tea to sit and enjoy, you remember an e-mail you didn't send and decide to write that as you absentmindedly sip from your mug. While getting away from devices entirely would be an incredibly radical and difficult thing to do these days, you can take a break from them.

Spend a couple of hours or, if you can, the whole day, without any devices, and commit yourself to spending that time as mindfully as you can. This includes noticing how many times your mind, or perhaps even your hand, goes to your phone.

What was this time like? What did you notice about your digital habits or perhaps even addiction?

....

....

....

....

....

....

A KOAN THAT GOES THE DISTANCE

This koan is attributed to the 13th-century Japanese monk Dō gen, who started the Sōtō school of Zen: "If there's even a hair's breadth of difference, heaven and earth are clearly separated. How do you understand that?" Koans were meant to make students of Zen doubt and think, to shake them out of old patterns of thought and approach things with a beginner's mind, with intuition instead of pure logic.

What do you think of when you ponder this koan? How, if at all, does it shake up your thinking?

....

....

....

....

....

....

....

....

"ONLY WHEN WE
IDENTIFY OURSELVES
WITH OTHERS CAN
WE GENUINELY ACT
WITH LOVE TOWARD
OTHERS."

–Kazuaki Tanahashi

COMPASSION CREATION

$\mathcal{A}$ natural part of embracing the oneness of creation is feeling compassion. The joy of others is your joy, the suffering of others is your suffering, and vice versa. Being compassionate doesn't mean you look out and judge others to be worthy of your pity, but instead you recognize the suffering around you and feel the desire to help. It creates action.

When have you received compassion?

....

....

....

....

....

....

....

....

....

continued . . .

When have you acted with compassion? How did it feel then, and how does it feel in your memory?

....

....

....

....

....

....

....

....

....

....

....

....

....

....

ZEN OUT COLORING

THAT MEANS YOU TOO

Compassion isn't only an outward thing. Self-compassion is as important as the compassion you have for others, but it can be the most difficult form of compassion of all. So often we're hard on ourselves and refuse to give ourselves the same charity and forgiveness we easily give to other people. Learning to be generous with self-compassion, though, opens you up to greater inner peace.

When have you shown yourself compassion, and when have you not?

....

....

....

....

....

....

....

....

What acts of compassion can you do for yourself?

....

....

....

....

....

....

....

....

....

....

....

CRACKING JOKES

*Z*en stories and koans often use humor as a teaching device. Laughter shows up in many Buddhist stories, even in, or perhaps especially in, dire situations, like when a monk is dying or dead. Being able to smile and laugh in any situation shows not only a deep understanding of Zen, but also a deep connection to the moment. You're not thinking of something else, worrying about the past or future. You're there, mindfully immersed in the moment.

What are some of your favorite jokes?

....

....

....

....

....

....

....

....

What are some of your best memories of laughing?

ZEN GARDENS

In Japan, outside Buddhist temples, you often find a garden created from stone and sand, and sometimes also water and plants, surrounded by walls on all but one side, where you'll find a platform to sit and contemplate the garden. These areas for reflection came to commonly be called Zen gardens.

Every aspect of the garden is purposefully designed. Large rocks and other elements such as water and plants stand in for the mountains, land, and rivers you find in nature. If the ground is covered with sand or gravel, it is raked into careful patterns, and the raked patterns are seen to represent rippling water. These days you can buy miniature versions of this kind of "dry garden" for your desk to rake in some Zen during your day.

No matter if the garden is large, intricate, and maintained outside a temple for centuries or a small desktop design, the purpose is the same. To mindfully care for the space and then to sit and contemplate how the garden is one and the same with the vastness of nature is to practice Zen.

ZEN OUT COLORING

ARE YOU LISTENING?

Have you ever been talking with someone and suspect that they just aren't hearing what you're saying, or maybe you're both missing each other? When you go into a conversation expecting to know what the other person thinks or feels, sometimes you don't actually hear what they're saying. Maybe you hear only what you want to hear, or maybe you expect them to argue or disagree with you and you hear what you *don't* want to hear even if that's not what they're trying to say. But if you use a beginner's mind in your interactions with other people, coming to them with no preconceptions and trying to see things from all angles, especially theirs, you might just get a surprise glimpse of their true nature.

Try talking with a beginner's mind to someone you know well, then write about how the conversation went. Did you make any discoveries or feel different than usual?

ZEN FLOW

One aim of Zen meditation is to connect to the moment, so you are absolutely present, doing only what you're doing, instead of having your mind drifting about as your body does something else. It can take active effort and concentration to achieve this kind of mindfulness when you're doing things like chores, but there is probably something you already do that puts you in this state, which is similar to what we often call "flow." When you're doing something you love—like yoga or singing or running or painting—sometimes the monkey mind quiets, the ego drops away, and you and what you're doing become one.

What activities put you in a state of flow? How does it feel when you're there?

....

....

....

....

....

....

"WE ARE WHAT WE THINK. ALL THAT WE ARE ARISES WITH OUR THOUGHTS. WITH OUR THOUGHTS WE MAKE THE WORLD."

–Siddhārtha Gautama, the Buddha

TURN ON THE LIGHT

These first lines of *The Dhammapada*, the most widely known collection of sayings of the Buddha, have been translated in many ways, but the meaning is usually understood the same way: your thoughts create your experience of the world.

If you think negative thoughts all the time, you'll experience the world negatively, but if you turn your mind on to the light of positive thoughts, then that's how the world will feel to you. And this goes beyond thoughts to what you say and what you do. As the verse continues: "Speak or act with an impure mind and trouble will follow you as the wheel follows the ox that draws the cart. . . . Speak or act with a pure mind and happiness will follow you as your shadow, unshakable."

What negative thoughts, words, or actions are you prone to?

....

....

....

....

....

....

continued . . .

How can you recast those negative thoughts, words, or actions so they turn into positives?

RESPECTFULLY YOURS

Respect is a core principle of Zen. How could it not be? If all is one, then everything and everyone deserves respect equally. This includes yourself, of course!

Following a zazen practice, one bows to the floor nine times, touching the forehead to the floor and lifting the palms of the hands. Bowing is a traditional show of respect. In zazen, however, it is a sign of respect toward not only Buddha but also the self—because you, yourself, are Buddha.

In what ways do you treat yourself with respect? Do you give yourself as much respect as you give others, or do you give yourself more or less? No matter what your answer, why do you think that is?

IT'S NOT ALWAYS EASY

Treating other people with equal respect isn't always easy, especially when they're people you don't agree with. On the other hand, it's easy to give more respect to people you, well, respect! This sort of judgment is something people are naturally inclined to do. Remembering that we're all in this together equally is one of the biggest challenges not just in traditional Zen but also in everyday life.

Meditate for a few minutes on the idea that we're all in this together and are deserving of equal respect. What feelings came up for you?

....

....

....

....

....

....

....

IT'S NOT *ONLY* NATURAL

The natural world is just as worthy of respect as people are. From plants and animals to inanimate objects, all things are connected. When you treat the world around you with reverence and respect, you give it the appreciation it deserves and you become more aware of how sacred and special all things are. The world begins to shine—or, more accurately, you start to become aware of how the world shines.

How can you show the natural world more respect? How do you think doing those things would change how you feel about nature?

REFLECT

ake some time to meditate on your *Zen Meditations Journal* journey so far. Think about how you approached life before you opened this book and how you approach life now.

Write about your experiences since you began this journal. Has anything changed for you, in your life, your mind, or your habits? Have you had any realizations or revelations? What intentions do you have for your journey forward?

....

....

....

....

....

....

....

....

....

A GRATEFUL WAY OF THINKING

One way to turn your mind to the present and nurture positive thinking is through gratitude. Thoughts often want to visit the past and what we once had or cast into the future for the things we want, but when you're actively grateful for what is great about the here and now, you become mindful of the present. And the more you bring your thoughts to gratitude, the more positivity you create.

What are you grateful for?

....

....

....

....

....

....

....

....

A CUPFUL OF KOAN

This koan dates back to a collection called Shasekishu (Sand and Pebbles), written by the Buddhist monk Mujū in the 13th century: A professor went to visit a master monk to ask about Zen. The monk began to pour tea for the professor, but once the cup was full he didn't stop pouring. The professor watched until he couldn't help but exclaim, "It is overfull. No more will go in!" The monk then told the professor that he was like the cup: he was full of his own ideas, saying "How can I show you Zen unless you first empty your cup?"

What ideas are you "overfull" with, meaning what are you so sure about that it would be very hard to fit in new ideas? How could you make a little room in your cup?

....

....

....

....

....

....

....

"GAIN OR LOSS, LET ME ACCEPT THE KARMA AS IT BRINGS TO ME THE ONE OR THE OTHER; THE MIND ITSELF KNOWS NEITHER INCREASE NOR DECREASE."

–D. T. Suzuki

WHAT IS, IS

When something difficult or unfair happens to you—for example, a cruel word is said to you or an accident happens—you can either get upset or choose acceptance. The former wastes your energy and generates negative thinking, while the second option is all around easier and more positive. It's the Zen way to work to change what can be changed and accept reality when things cannot be changed. It is a bit like the Serenity Prayer, which prays for the ability to accept what can't be changed, the courage to change what can be changed, and the wisdom to know the difference.

What unalterable reality are you upset about and maybe wasting energy trying to change?

....

....

....

....

....

....

....

continued . . .

Write an acceptance letter to this reality, letting go of the negative feelings you've been holding on to.

SHOULD YOU REALLY?

*Y*ou can shake yourself out of some old negative habits of thinking and doing by changing how you talk to yourself about your actions. So often we say to ourselves that "I should do" something or "I should have done" something. All this "should-ing" implies that we know the right thing to do. It implies judgment and even some self-blame. Instead of telling yourself what you *should* do, what if you told yourself what you *could do*?

Try this out. Think of something from your to-do list, maybe something that's been on there for a long time and you really feel like you should do it. Write about how you could do it, or you could do something else. Use your beginner's mind to explore as many options and outcomes as you can.

LET'S BE HONEST

*D*oes anything feel less Zen than lying? When you're dishonest, you get that squirmy, unsettling feeling that makes your mind go over and over the lie and all the negative things it implies about you. It just feels bad. The truth, on the other hand, though sometimes really difficult to force off your tongue, feels cleansing, freeing, like a weight lifting, the air clearing, light shining, and many other poetic, positive similes.

What does a lie feel like to you? What about the truth?

....

....

....

....

....

....

....

....

KEEPING THE PEACE

Zen is all about finding peace, within and without. It's only natural, then, that refraining from violence is an essential part of peace. Violence is, after all, the opposite of peace. It's negativity in action. In Buddhism, nonviolence is a core principle that applies not just to other people but also to animals, the environment, and most certainly the self. (Nonviolence is not identical to peace because it allows for disruption and social change through peaceful acts.)

How could you be more peaceful or nonviolent?

....

....

....

....

....

....

....

....

ZEN ALTARS

Creating an altar in the space where you meditate has many benefits. It can act as a focal point for your meditation, serve as a reminder of your aspirations and what is dear to you, and generate a spiritual atmosphere.

Often, altars will have a statue of the Buddha and pictures of loved ones or spiritual figures. Some altars have water, flowers, incense, a lit candle, perfume, food, and music. But there are no hard-and-fast rules for setting up a Zen altar. If something feels special to you and gives you that sense of the sacred, you can include it.

The space itself should be kept tidy and free of dust. If you burn incense, the ashes should be cleared away. A satisfying altar is often one that strikes a good balance—it isn't cluttered, but it isn't too spare. It feels just right.

What would you include on your altar?

Draw your ideal Zen altar below.

FROM THE ORDINARY
TO THE SACRED

In Zen, anything and everything can become a ritual. Brushing your teeth, sweeping, gardening, bathing, dressing, cooking, eating—all these tasks can be made sacred if you do them with mindful devotion. Maybe you even have some rituals already, like lighting candles when you take a bath or saying grace before you eat. But special tasks and tools are not needed to live your life as a continuous practice. All that needs to be done is to practice zazen and understand that to fully express your nature is to express Buddha nature.

What rituals do you already have? What are some you'd like to create?

A KILLER KOAN

One of the most famous koans of all comes from the 9th-century Chinese Buddhist monk Linji Yixuan, who is supposed to have said this to his students: "If you meet the Buddha on the road, kill him." For a nonviolent group, this is a pretty jarring statement, which is exactly what koans are supposed to be. They are not logic puzzles; they are intuition ignitions meant to bring you to a new level of understanding.

Meditate for a few minutes on this koan, then free-write what comes to mind.

....

....

....

....

....

....

....

....

EXPECT THE UNEXPECTED

*Y*ou can only ever be disappointed if you have an expectation in the first place. If you fully expect that something will happen or go a certain way, and it doesn't pan out, you'll be let down. If you think someone should do something or behave a certain way but then they don't, you'll likely get bummed out or annoyed.

But if instead you don't expect things to turn out a certain way, then you won't have unmet expectations. If you let go of your attachments and allow the world to be the mysterious and often baffling place it truly is instead of putting your own narrative on it, you can get that much closer to understanding and embracing the true nature of things. This doesn't mean you never think of what might happen; it just means you try to avoid becoming attached to what you think *should* happen.

What expectations are you currently holding on to? Write them down and then cross them out as you meditate on letting them go.

....

....

....

....

....

....

LETTING GO

Most of us are attached to the world, meaning we respond to who and what is around us, going from positive to negative depending on circumstances. Nonattachment, on the other hand, is a key (albeit tricky) concept in Zen that aims to turn inward for your sense of well-being. Reality is what it is, and while you are present and aware of it, you don't become upset by it. You accept that what is, is in the outside world, and inwardly you are at peace. This doesn't mean you can't experience joy or love; it simply means your experience of those things is dependent on the steady peace within rather than on the ever-changing world around you.

Contemplate this idea of nonattachment for a few minutes. What do you think of it? Does it seem doable to you in any measure?

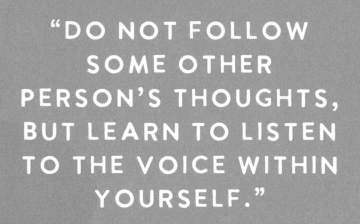

"DO NOT FOLLOW SOME OTHER PERSON'S THOUGHTS, BUT LEARN TO LISTEN TO THE VOICE WITHIN YOURSELF."

–Dōgen

ZEN AND NOW

Now that you have taken the entire journey of this journal, you have likely learned and experienced some things that serve you and others that don't. Some things felt right and true, while others, not so much. To find your own path, you must learn to hear your own voice, and in one of the great ironies of Zen, once you truly find yourself, you forget yourself as you unite with the oneness of all things.

Take some time to go back through what you've written in this journal. What, if anything, has changed for you in your life, your mind, or your habits since you started?

....

....

....

....

....

....

....

....

continued . . .

What intentions do you have for your Zen journey going forward?

Hay House Titles of Related Interest

Evening Meditations Journal,
by The Hay House Editors

The Gift of Gratitude: A Guided Journal for Counting Your Blessings,
by Louise Hay

The High 5 Daily Journal,
by Mel Robbins

Living Your Purpose Journal,
by Dr. Wayne W. Dyer

Morning Meditations Journal,
by The Hay House Editors

The Sacred Cycles Journal,
by Jill Pyle, Em Dewey, and Cidney Bachert

Sweet Dreams Journal,
by The Hay House Editors

All of the above are available at your local bookstore,
or may be ordered by contacting Hay House (see next page).

* * *

We hope you enjoyed this Hay House book. If you'd like to receive our online catalog featuring additional information on Hay House books and products, or if you'd like to find out more about the Hay Foundation, please contact:

Hay House, Inc., P.O. Box 5100, Carlsbad, CA 92018-5100
(760) 431-7695 or (800) 654-5126
(760) 431-6948 (fax) or (800) 650-5115 (fax)
www.hayhouse.com® • www.hayfoundation.org

———

Published in Australia by: Hay House Australia Pty. Ltd.,
18/36 Ralph St., Alexandria NSW 2015
Phone: 612-9669-4299 • *Fax:* 612-9669-4144
www.hayhouse.com.au

Published in the United Kingdom by: Hay House UK, Ltd.,
The Sixth Floor, Watson House, 54 Baker Street, London W1U 7BU
Phone: +44 (0)20 3927 7290 • *Fax:* +44 (0)20 3927 7291
www.hayhouse.co.uk

Published in India by: Hay House Publishers India,
Muskaan Complex, Plot No. 3, B-2, Vasant Kunj, New Delhi 110 070
Phone: 91-11-4176-1620 • *Fax:* 91-11-4176-1630
www.hayhouse.co.in

———

Access New Knowledge.
Anytime. Anywhere.

Learn and evolve at your own pace
with the world's leading experts.

www.hayhouseU.com

SOURCES

Page 10: *Zen Mind, Beginner's Mind*, Shunryu Suzuki, edited by Trudy Dixon. New York: Weatherhill, 1993.

Page 22: *Commit to Sit: Tools for Cultivating a Meditation Practice*, Joan Duncan Oliver. New York: Hay House, 2009.

Page 36: *Old Path White Clouds: Walking in the Footsteps of the Buddha*, Thich Nhat Hanh. Berkeley, CA: Parallax Press, 1987.

Page 48: *How to Eat*, Thich Nhat Hanh. Berkeley, CA: Parallax Press, 2014.

Page 56: *Zen Mind, Beginner's Mind,* Shunryu Suzuki, edited by Trudy Dixon. New York: Weatherhill, 1993.

Page 72: *Treasury of the True Dharma Eye: Zen Master Dogen's Shobo Genzo*, Kazuaki Tanahashi. Boulder, CO: Shambhala, 2013.

Page 86: Siddhārtha Gautama, the Buddha, *The Dhammapada: The Sayings of the Buddha.* New York: Crown Publishing Group, 2001.

Page 100: *Manual of Zen Buddhism*, Daisetz Teitaro Suzuki. New York: Grove Press, 1994.

Page 120: *Buddhism and Zen*, Nyogen Senzaki. New York: North Point Press, 1988.

HAY HOUSE
Online Video Courses

Your journey to a better life starts with figuring out which path is best for you. Hay House Online Courses provide guidance in mental and physical health, personal finance, telling your unique story, and so much more!

LEARN HOW TO:

- choose your words and actions wisely so you can tap into life's magic

- clear the energy in yourself and your environments for improved clarity, peace, and joy

- forgive, visualize, and trust in order to create a life of authenticity and abundance

- manifest lifelong health by improving nutrition, reducing stress, improving sleep, and more

- create your own unique angelic communication toolkit to help you to receive clear messages for yourself and others

- use the creative power of the quantum realm to create health and well-being

To find the guide for your journey,
visit www.HayHouseU.com.

HAY HOUSE
online learning